VICTORY IN THE GULF

Eric Micheletti & Yves Debay

Windrow & Greene

SEVEN MONTHS WHICH MAY CHANGE THE WORLD

At 1.30 a.m. on 2 August 1990 a telephone rang in the quarters of Prince Sa'ad Abdallah, Prime Minister of Kuwait. The Minister of Defense was shouting down the line : hundreds of Iraqi tanks had crossed the frontier and were racing towards Kuwait City. The Second Gulf War had begun. Five days later the United States launched Operation 'Desert Shield'.

On 3 March 1991, militarily routed, the representatives of Iraqi dictator Saddam Hussein formally recognized the United Nations Security Council resolution laying down terms for a cease-fire. Her military, industrial, and economic infrastructure smashed to rubble, two thirds of her army destroyed, and a huge swathe of her territory occupied, Iraq had lost the war.

Those seven months had perhaps changed the world for a generation ahead. An almost total military blockade had been enforced against the aggressor. Half a million troops had been massed along a huge desert frontier and in a vast logistic network supporting it. Six weeks of air attack, and a ground war lasting just 100 hours, had humbled the fourth largest army in the world. A coalition which no one had believed possible, embracing nations divided by suspicion for decades, held together throughout those seven months despite enormous political pressures. More : the troops of many of these nations had served side by side — in a land previously almost forbidden to Westerners except under the most stringent limitations — and had finally fought together.

To achieve this result a gigantic 'bridge' of air and sea transport had been constructed in a few weeks and maintained for many months. No comparable logistic achievement has been seen since World War II nearly half a century ago. Even for the USA, the richest and strongest nation on earth, 'Desert Shield' remains the supreme example of military deployment in terms of time and volume.

This was officially a United Nations war, undertaken with the consent of most of the world community — even that of the USSR. Yet its day-to-day conduct lay in the hands of the USA, in the persons of Chairman of the Joint Chiefs Gen. Colin Powell and the commander of US Central Command, Gen. H. Norman Schwarzkopf; and — once and for all — they have laid to rest the ghosts of Vietnam. As the months passed there was no shortage of pundits to spread alarm about the thousands of allied personnel who would inevitably die in the attempt to recapture Saddam's pretended fortress in occupied Kuwait. In the event Operation 'Desert Storm' was a total success, achieved at a cost in allied lives so low it can only be termed miraculous. This magnificent victory confirmed not only the superiority of Western technology, but also the courage of allied servicemen and women, and their willingness to do the job, whatever the risks, until victory is achieved.

Despite their huge numerical strength, deployed on relatively short interior lines, Baghdad's forces proved quite unable to resist Western superiority of equipment, professionalism and discipline to any meaningful degree. And Saddam's soldiers knew it : abandoned by their commanders, cut off from the most basic supplies, their response to the allied advance was to surrender in their tens of thousands.

Apart from its immediate significance for the participating powers, this war may well mark a historic turning-point. We may at least hope that it heralds the chance of a wholly new level of international co-operation; and that the Middle East may, in time, be rescued from its past role as the cockpit for surrogate conflict between East and West. That the USA can take credit for a courageous and generous lead in this attempt will be denied by few.

ARRIVAL

Vaguely muzzy after a dozen hours cooped up inside an aircraft, or bored after a fortnight pacing the confines of a transport ship, the soldiers of 'Desert Shield' gazed around them at the strange land — the holy ground of one of the world's great religions — where they had come to fight. Bellowed orders half-heard above the constant roar of engines directed them and their newly sand-painted vehicles to the huge transit camps, and from there out into the deep desert.

During their journey to Saudi Arabia they had already been taught something of the life of this new culture, and told how to avoid offending the local population. The essential lessons of life in the desert had been dinned into them —

the first being to drink, and keep drinking. They had been taught how to recognize allies from enemies — no simple task in a coalition of this size. They had a lot to learn and remember; as things turned out, they would have long months to assimilate the lessons, but in those early days they did not know that.

Throughout the first two months, as huge transport jets landed and took off in an unending procession, and cargo and troop ships tied up and discharged their loads in a single day, everything was new and strange. The GIs' boots hardly had time to hit the hot tarmac or the quayside before they were chivvied into fleets of commandeered tourist or school buses and headed out into a landscape of crushing emptiness.

Previous page :
The gigantic 'air bridge' constructed by the USA rested principally on hundreds of transports of the Military Airlift Command. Huge C-5A Galaxy aircraft carried out a shuttle over half the globe, and by mid-August a heavy transport was landing in Arabia every five minutes. A never-ending flood of men and material poured out onto the tarmac of Dhahran in the north east of the kingdom.

Top :
From the rail of the USS *Anderson* arriving in the port of Damman, drivers of the 180th Transport Battalion take their first look at Saudi Arabia.

Bottom :
The ubiquitous 'Humvee' — the US forces' all-terrain, all-purpose light vehicle — rolls ashore from a US fast transport ship; this one is fitted with a Stinger missile rig.

Opposite :
The USS *Bellatrix* empties her holds of the Bradley armored carriers of the 24th Infantry Division. In less than six weeks, the equipment for five divisions had been landed in-country.

Previous page :
Saturday 20 October 1990, 11.00 hours : the 'Greys' roll ashore from the transport *Sir Bedivere*. The Challenger tanks of the Royal Scots Dragoon Guards are the spearhead of Britain's 7th Armoured Brigade, who wear the World War II shoulder patch of the 7th Armoured Division — the 'Desert Rats' who fought Rommel in the Libyan desert.

Top left :
An American 'beachmaster', settled in to the months-long task of supervising the arrival of men, machines and material aboard civil and military transports in the ports of Damman and Al Jubayl. The US divisions are quickly moved out of the crowded port areas and north towards the frontier 200 miles away, where the Iraqi army is digging in.

Bottom left :
Dwarfed by its huge maritime flock, a tiny US Coast Guard patrol vessel at Damman keeps watch for possible Iraqi commando raids from the sea.

Right :
In the rapid deployment from the USA and Europe many allied troops arrived before supplies of desert camouflage uniform were available. Still clad in green jungle battledress, a British 'Tom' waits to disembark.

Top :
Deposited by a 24-hour-a-day 'cab-rank' of Galaxies, Starlifters and DC-10s on the tarmac at Dhahran, GIs and Marines were moved out to a tented camp on the edge of the desert, and ordered to drink a litre and a half of bottled water inside two hours. The Western soldier would quickly learn to respect the Arabian sun.

Bottom :
Laden, but confident, the 18th Aviation Brigade head from the aircraft to a convoy of chartered buses for their journey out to their unit bases.

Opposite :
Yanbu, 1 October : his green beret and silver grenade badges identify a trooper of the French Foreign Legion's 1er REC (1st Foreign Cavalry Regiment), equipped with AMX-10 RC heavy armored cars. His tattoo marks him as an 'Anglo-Saxon'; his attitude, as a hard-bitten professional.

Overleaf :
The first combat units of the French 'Daguet' Division prepare to head out of Yanbu into the deep desert. The fast, heavily armed and armored AMX-10 RC is for all intents and purposes a wheeled light tank, operating alongside VAB armored personnel carriers; the armor is supported by supply trucks and P-4 light vehicles.

Opposite :
The troopers of the US 'First Cav' arrived some days previously by air, to begin their acclimatisation. Now fast transport ships deliver their mounts. The remarkable logistic organisation of 'Desert Shield' succeeded in moving entire units, with all equipment, from the States to Arabia in just sixteen days.

Overleaf :
Weeks of acclimatisation were needed before most US units were truly combat-ready in these extreme conditions; although some had recently trained in the California desert, many were shocked by their rapid delivery from temperate climates to the baking wastes of Arabia. Quickest to get to grips with the new challenge were the paratroopers of the 82nd Airborne Division, already deployed by mid-August.

THE BUILD-UP

The setting in place of some 600,000 servicemen and women from the 29 countries of the anti-Iraqi coalition would test the organisational skills of the Western armies to their limits, but would not find them wanting. The projection of such enormous resources over tens of thousands of miles was perhaps the most dazzling of all the allies' achievements; and it was carried out without degrading the operational readiness of either personnel or equipment — even the most delicate electronics. By the outbreak of hostilities the total air and sea movements to the Gulf are estimated at some 58 million miles.

While the operational capabilities of the armies, navies and air forces of 'Desert Shield' and 'Desert Storm' attract the most immediate attention, it should not be forgotten that they could not have been brought to bear with any hope of success without this massively competent logistical exercise. The actual fighting men represented only a minority of the total. Scores of thousands of men and women working flat-out in the rear areas were necessary to feed the coalition's insatiable daily appetite for rations, water, fuel, ammunition, and every one of the hundred items of equipment needed to keep units operational.

Saudi Arabia herself contributed huge amounts of water, fuel, and rations, and the services of thousands of vehicles and dozens of repair shops; the kingdom was supplying the US forces with 16 million gallons of fuel every day.

To build up and maintain the 60 days' stocks of every necessity which General Schwarzkopf insisted upon required the creation and orchestration of a ceaseless river of convoy and helicopter movements. Some five million tons of equipment were shipped to the Gulf, and another 450,000 tons were air-lifted. Much of this total had to be moved out of the port and airfield facilities and forward to the rear-echelon camps of the fighting formations. The military police of the allied armies performed miracles of co-ordination to keep this metal flood moving in the right directions, on schedule. It is calculated that the coalition had one vehicle for between every two and three soldiers in-country.

This bewildering pattern of activity did not slacken off for a moment. With the announcement in November that large additional US, and some additional British and French forces were to be committed to the Gulf, the pace even quickened.

Allied troops faced with operations in a multi-national coalition were quick to display their flags. During the build-up phase it was a useful administrative identification, and a soldierly gesture of pride; once the shooting started, it was sometimes a matter of life or death.

Tradition is important to soldiers anywhere; in the field, it is an essential element of unit pride and confidence.

Top left :
In a featureless wilderness half a world from home, the colors of a US airborne unit are paraded for a change of command. Wherever they are sent, whatever their mission, the unit's heart is wherever the colors fly.

Bottom left :
A new generation of British soldiers get to mark the jaunty red jerboa of 7th Armoured on sand-painted steel — and on this particular vehicle the desert rat is associated with a name recalling past glories.

Opposite :
The Foreign Legion's reverence for tradition is legendary. Here the 1st Foreign Cavalry parade their pennant, wearing the white képis and fringed epaulettes echoing a hundred and fifty years of desert campaigns.

Top left :
The ever-reliable Chinook, workhorse of the US Army since Vietnam, lands on a desert DZ. US forces deployed hundreds of helicopters to the Gulf, and not only for logistic support : the daring airborne advance by thousands of 101st Airborne 'Screaming Eagles' in hundreds of choppers, to set a self-sufficient blocking force across the rear of the Iraqi army in Kuwait, was a modern parallel to the massed parachute drops of World War II.

Bottom left :
Britain's 7th Armoured Brigade at first took up positions with the US Marines on the coast, providing the Leathernecks with heavier armored punch. Later the reinforced British 1st Armoured Division, 25,000 strong, was moved north-west to fight under US VII Corps in the 'left hook' against Saddam's tank reserves.

Opposite :
The 'All Americans' install their artillery — the M102 105mm howitzer, powerful but highly manoeuvrable, can be lifted under a helicopter and flown anywhere on the battlefield at short notice.

Fashions in headgear : what the desert soldier is wearing this year...

Top left :
The 'boonie' may not be stylish, but style is not uppermost in the minds of these 2nd Division Marines, for whom a break in exercises means just another few thousand sandbags to fill.

Bottom left :
The workaday bone-dome of a US tanker, ready for action at a moment's notice.

Top right :
Neatly aligned on the track of their self-propelled M109, the 'Fritz' lightweight combat helmets of a crew from 41st Field Artillery, far from their usual base at Babenhausen in Germany.

Bottom right :
The practical French army desert scarf or *chèche* protects the légionnaire from sun and dust; it is also, undeniably, *très folklorique*!

Opposite :
**Last chance to bone up for
a Marine killing time at the
Dhahran reception area.**

DAILY ROUTINE

The desert may seem timeless, but the GIs and Marines were given little chance for metaphysical reflection. Six days out of every seven they trained, and trained hard. General Schwarzkopf warned his units that they should get used to the idea of an operation lasting six months at least, and even longer before they saw their homes and families again. It was not easy for troops lifted straight from bases in the United States or long-established 'homes away from home' in Germany to get used to the isolation of desert camps, or the unseen but real weight of Islamic traditions which imposed so many constraints on their behaviour.

In this baking emptiness the US forces performed prodigies of improvisation to help the troops' morale. It was a hotter, dustier, lonelier place than many of them had ever imagined; and just when they learned to cope with the heat and dust, it turned wet and freezing. But for one precious day each week most of them could look forward to a visit to a 'leisure center'. In sober truth this was simply a large tented camp in the middle of nothing; but they could read, and lounge in the shade, or play sports, or watch movies. Perhaps best of all, there were hundreds of satellite-link telephones, so they could call their families at home. At Thanksgiving and Christmas the lines stretched out of sight.

For the British troops the conditions came as just as much of a novelty; few British units these days have been nearer to a real desert than the parched training area of Suffield in Canada. Still, they quickly established the kind of small domestic routines which bind a British battalion into a self-protective family; and although often cynical about media hype, many took a quiet satisfaction in serving in an environment so intimately associated with Britain's WW II military traditions. It was, after all, 'marvellous tank country'.

For the French contingent this aspect was also important for morale; the Foreign Legion was born in Africa and fought in deserts for most of its first 130 years. Even today légionnaires are frequently rotated for training — or active service — through desert postings like Chad and Djibouti; and for the younger men to get sand in their boots was a real satisfaction. Their camps were among the most isolated of all; their rota of combat and chemical warfare exercises, as relentless as any. But even in the desert some standards are sacred : allied visitors reported that the food in the Daguet Division's lines was unbelievable!

Previous page :
Only the American soldier can show such determination to transplant a vision of home comforts into the middle of a sun-parched hell. The 'Beach Club' was the work of the 'Battlekings' of the 69th Tank Battalion, 24th Infantry Division (Mechanized).

Top left :
Water, as much as fuel, was what this war ran on, and it was guarded like treasure. One of the reasons for the ultimate collapse of the Iraqi units in the front line was their army's failure to keep water supplies on the move during the allied air campaign.

Bottom left, top right :
The US command was constantly vigilant against the danger of water shortages, and enforced water discipline. For several days after their first arrival, GIs were ordered to drink one and a half litres inside two hours — and to keep on doing it. While no serious shortage ever occured, not much could be said for the taste of the stuff when it had been quietly boiling in a man's canteen for a few hours of desert manoeuvres.

Bottom right :
French soldiers halt on the march to damp down the dust. The beer, sadly, is non-alcoholic, in deference to Saudi religious principles.

34

Top left :
Desert or no desert, certain aspects of the American way of life were scrupulously preserved; in this tented mini-PX the troopers of the '24th Mech' could still find their favorite cookies and candy.

Bottom left :
The justly legendary US talent for logistics won new fame in the Gulf; even at the humble level of this open-air cookhouse belonging to the 82nd Aviation Brigade, it was impressive. In the background, OH-58 Kiowa helicopters.

Opposite :
USAF airmen at Dhahran square up to bacon and beans, perhaps the US military's most enduring tradition of all.

'We got volleyball and baseball, and a lotta fancy games....'
For six months the GIs lived like monks; the local culture demanded it, and they only had one day a week off, anyway. Sports were organised wherever practical, to help keep the men sharp during the long, uncertain months of waiting for something to happen.

Top left :
A rest facility of the '24th Mech', October 1990.

Bottom left :
Tankers of the 1st Marine Expeditionary Force improvise a diamond beside their M60A1s in the front line just a few days before the land war broke out.

Opposite :
A Marine and his best friend use slack time wisely in a transit camp.

Top left :
A veteran once remarked on the amount of waste paper blowing about a battlefield. Modern soldiers know why.... a technician of the 82nd Airborne's Aviation Brigade pores over yet another of the interminable check-lists.

Bottom left :
Strategy in the sand : Marines get to see how it feels to be the one moving the pawns, for a change.

Opposite :
At the 82nd Aviation Brigade's Hufuf base a female paratrooper loses herself for precious moments in a letter from home.

THE MEN AND THE WEAPONS

The coalition's superiority in weapons had to be total : that decision was taken in the White House during the first days of the crisis. General Colin Powell, Chairman of the Joint Chiefs, headed a Pentagon team dedicated to one aim : if it came to war, the allies would hit hard and fast, with everything they had. General Scharzkopf had a free hand in assembling whatever means he wanted in the Gulf. That was the only way to keep allied casualties to a minimum; and it was widely believed that Western electorates would not tolerate a long-drawn, costly war.

There was to be no grudging of equipment for the Gulf; units and depots were ruthlessly stripped to ensure that the expeditionary forces had the best, in abundance.

The US and British armies in Germany sent their most modern Abrams and Challenger tanks. Divisions received more artillery and engineer assets than their normal establishment. Reservists were recalled from civilian life if their specialties were required — particularly medical personnel. The USAF sent its F-15 Eagles, its B-52 strategic bombers, even its latest F-117 'Stealth' fighters to bases in Saudi Arabia, other Gulf states, and the Indian Ocean. Britain combined her best RAF aircrews into composite squadrons of Tornado low-level bombers. Six US Navy carrier groups would eventually take station in the Red Sea and the Gulf — as would two of the recommissioned World War II battleships which now mounted not only mighty turret guns, but dozens of ultra-accurate Tomahawk cruise missiles. The untried Patriot anti-missile system was deployed to guard against Saddam's Scuds. The terrible Apache helicopter, the most modern attack chopper in the world, would be targeted on Iraq's large tank army, and with it the massively strong and dangerous A-10 tank-busting jet.

This was not to be a confrontation of machinery versus men, either. The fighting troops sent into the desert would be the very best : the US paratroopers and Marines, the British 'Desert Rats' and French Foreign Legion were the pick of the West's professional, volunteer warriors.

And though their missions were, and will remain, shrouded in secrecy, it is calculated that some 3,500 Special Forces from the allied armies operated deep behind enemy lines from long before the shooting war started — one allied officer has said that they turned large areas of Iraq into a Special Forces theme park...

Previous page :
The world gathered around its TV screens, arguing about threatening politico-military scenarios, discovered a new metal hero straight out of *Star Wars* : the Patriot anti-missile, guardian of the night skies over Saudi Arabia and Israel. This four-pack launcher served with the 11th Air Defense Artillery Brigade.

Any gallery of 'GI portraits' from now on must include not only representatives of Afro-American and Hispanic minorities — who are more significantly represented in the service than in the civilian population — but also of servicewomen. At least ten per cent of the American forces in the Gulf were female; several — their duties taking them inescapably into harm's way — gave their lives, and others were briefly captured, though returning apparently unharmed after the allied victory.

Previous page :
The M270 Multiple-Launch Rocket System is another new weapon which proved massively effective in the hands of US and British artillery units, inflicting great damage on Iraqi positions in the week leading up to the ground offensive and on troop concentrations during the fighting. This tracked launcher served with 'First Cav'. The twelve 13-foot rockets are unguided but extremely accurate, with a range of some 18 miles. They can be fired in various sequences, including a full salvo; and each M77 warhead scatters 644 sub-munitions. A salvo can devastate an area of many hundreds of square yards in a matter of seconds.

For years the West has prepared for the 'air-land battle' — the indivisibly co-ordinated use of ground forces with helicopter and fixed-wing air assets in the destruction of enemy armor and artillery. 'Desert Storm' would be the first time it had been tested on a large scale in actual combat.

Top left :
The uncertain but chilling threat of Iraqi chemical weapons was never far from the allied command's calculations when facing a dictator who had killed 5,000 of his own citizens in a single chemical strike. Groundcrew practice decontaminating an AH-1 Cobra helicopter.

Bottom left :
Refuelling a Gazelle attack helicopter attached to the French contingent.

Opposite :
The face of the predator. This Cobra is armed with four TOW guided anti-tank missiles with a range of two miles; 38 unguided 2.75in. Hydra rockets; and a rotary 20mm cannon.

Top left :
The desert is no novelty for the Foreign Legion, which has seen active service in Chad in recent years. Nevertheless, the Legion cavalry were under no illusions about their mission : Iraqi T-72s would likely be a different proposition from Libyan T-55s and Cascavels.

Bottom left :
Two worlds meet — a little tentative, always puzzled, but bound by the recognition of mutual need. Perhaps Saddam has done some good for the world, despite himself?

Opposite :
The 45,000 British personnel of 1st Armoured Division and its many supporting units included virtually every cap-badge in the British army — including that of a Gurkha support regiment. The centuries old regimental 'tribalism' of the British proved no barrier to rapid cross-postings to bring units up to a full war strength for the Gulf. The squaddies riding a single APC might prove to include men of three different battalions, operating as a harmonious team.

TRAINING

The great majority of the coalition troops had some months to adapt themselves to the hostile environment of the desert; and to prepare themselves for what would be — in terms of the numbers of men and the sheer volume of materiel involved — one of the greatest battles in history. Moreover, before even setting foot on the sands of Arabia many of the American troops had already had the opportunity to practice desert combat techniques at the National Training Center at Fort Irwin in the Mojave desert of California. Since 1982 about 400,000 American troops have passed through the center, learning to make the unique conditions of the world's deserts work for them — both in the heat of day and, significantly, in the cold darkness of the night.

Even so, the US high command in Saudi Arabia was determined that there was no such thing as too much training. They were particularly dedicated to practising the movement of troops with the minimum of impedimenta, and the corollary which was therefore inescapable : the establishment of an absolutely reliable logistics network. Fast movement meant carrying the minimum of supplies and spares, which meant that resupply at short notice was vital. And over the whole program hung the threat — often brandished by Saddam Hussein during the second half of 1990 — of chemical warfare. The troopers had to spend hours at a time, day after day, in NBC suits and gasmasks; and they had to learn how to stay sharp despite these handicaps.

For the US Marines the classic amphibious landing occupied much training time off-shore and on the beaches of Saudi Arabia. The question of whether or not such a landing would be made in earnest was one of the great strategic riddles in the run-up to war — and the Iraqis were deliberately encouraged to believe it would be, thus tying down divisions along the Kuwaiti coast.

The training of all the coalition armies, and particularly the Western troops, centred above all on the assault : getting through minefields and barbed wire, clearing trenches, and storming enemy bunkers with grenade and bayonet... The simultaneous need to patrol the frontier zone, mapping waterholes, Bedouin camps and enemy advanced positions, ensured that time would not hang heavy in the months before battle.

Previous page :
Fifteen days before this photograph was taken, the Warrior mechanised infantry combat vehicles of the 1st Bn., The Staffordshire Regiment (the British equivalent to the US Bradley) arrived direct from the muddy plains of Germany.

Top left :
Practice in crossing an anti-tank ditch for the 197th Infantry Brigade (Mechanized)(Separate) of the US XVIII Airborne Corps. The 'Forever Forward' brigade lived up to its name in February 1991, striking deep into Iraq. The M113 APC — though up-graded in many respects since the Vietnam war — is still in widespread service in some mechanized units.

Bottom left :
Elderly, but still useful as a fast 'battlefield hack', a Ferret scout car of the British 7th Armoured Brigade speeds over the desert.

Right :
Légionnaire of the 2nd Foreign Infantry Regiment reporting in during a reconnaissance by VAB wheeled APC of the Daguet Division. The division was a task force assembled specifically for the Gulf operation, headed up by units of France's Rapid Action Force drawn from the 6th Light Armored Division, a permanent formation.

Overleaf :
By the turn of the year the M1A1 Abrams tanks of the 'First Cav' had been in-country two months. Confident that they crewed the best tank in the world, the troopers were impatient to find out what Saddam's armored units were made of; in the event, they proved good judges.

Above :
Thirty years on, and still trucking... a Huey of the 101st Airborne Division (Air Assault) on a supply mission.

Right :
Abrasive sand, talcum-fine dust, and heat all posed a threat to sensitive ultra-high technology systems and constant checks were necessary to maintain a high state of readiness for combat. Here an AH-64 Apache attack helicopter, the fangs of the 82nd Aviation Brigade, is temporarily sheltered with a parachute canopy.

Opposite :
A cliché from a Hollywood Western serves as an all too real reminder of the desert's lack of mercy for Challenger tank crews of the Royal Scots Dragoon Guards.

Above :
Hazed by heat and dust, a Warrior infantry carrier bursts over a sand berm under the hovering protection of a TOW-equipped Lynx helicopter of the British 1st Armoured Division.

Right :
Challenger of the Queen's Royal Irish Hussars, hull-down on a sand dune, provides flank protection for a mechanized infantry battalion; in the foreground, a signals 'track';

Top right :
A British MP with motorcycle scouts of an armored field ambulance unit.

Top left :
Anti-tank team from the Foreign Legion's 2nd Infantry practising with their battle-proven Milan missile launcher near Hafar al Batin. Despite the low profile of most modern anti-tank weapons for the infantry, the problem of concealment is very real in desert as flat as a pool table.

Bottom left :
First you train; then you train some more; then you do it all over.... Marines of the 1st MEF leap from their LAV fast armored reconnaissance vehicle to practice taking out an enemy strongpoint after an initial penetration of the front line defenses, under cover of the turret-mounted 25mm 'chain-gun.'

Opposite :
Paratrooper RTO checking in his platoon's position; a navigation error in this featureless landscape is easy — but it could bring down a salvo of allied shellfire, or a rain of horror from the sky above.

Overleaf :
Apache country, 1990s style... and under the baleful gaze of the US Army's AH-64, it's as dangerous as it ever was in the days of Geronimo. Cruising easily at nearly 200 mph, the Apache mounts a 30mm 'Gatling gun' rotary cannon and a powerful mix of rockets; it can carry up to 16 Hellfire laser-homing anti-tank missiles with a range of nearly four miles. During the third week of February, when the coalition forces were softening up Iraqi advanced positions on the eve of the land offensive, some hundreds of Iraqi infantry actually surrendered to hovering Apaches.

Top left : **a British Warrior infantry combat vehicle rolls north-west towards the VII Corps jumping off-line.**

Below : **two kinds of versatile desert transport, separated by a few tens of thousands of years but apparently able to co-exist : a Humvee excites little reaction from a camel herd.**

Overleaf : **Marines of the 3rd Recon, 1st MEF. While a second huge Marine force cruised menacingly off-shore, threatening Saddam with a classic amphibious operation and tying down his divisions along the Kuwaiti coast, the Leathernecks were in fact preparing for a straight frontal thrust which would smash through enemy lines to the outskirts of Kuwait City in 48 hours. The weapon here is the M249 Squad Automatic Weapon, which has replaced the M60 in the infantry fire team.**

A French Marine non-com of the 11th RAMa relaxes — watchfully — in the hatch of his VAB. Desert camo helmet covers and body armor arrived before full camouflage uniforms.

Top left :
M113s of the 197th Infantry Brigade practice penetrating an enemy minefield. Saddam was known to have a huge arsenal of many different types, including some which are virtually undetectable. Gen. Schwarzkopf — who has personal experience — took the threat with deadly seriousness.

Bottom left :
US Marines bowed beneath the weight of their packs — and the pitiless desert sun — rendezvous with a huge CH-53 Stallion helicopter at the end of a battle exercise.

Top right :
Légionnaires trudge up a sand dune under the weight of the Milan launcher and rounds, for the hundredth time.

Bottom right :
An RAF Puma lands a tank-killer team from the 1st Bn., Staffordshire Rgt in the deep desert.

Previous page :
The backbone of the allied artillery : the M109 self-propelled 155mm howitzer, with a range of up to 15 miles with rocket-assisted ammunition. It has a speed of up to 35 mph, and can cover 220 miles without refuelling. 'Alcatraz' is the dangerous mobile home of six gunners from the '24th Mech's' 41st Field Artillery Brigade, Battery F.

Top left :
Airborne tankers of one of the 82nd's Sheridan crews, tired and cold after a winter night manoeuvre.

Bottom left :
US MP bikers in a desert encampment.

Top right :
Fire orders for French Marine gunners of the 11th RAMa, their TRF-1 pieces emplaced at the far west of the coalition line facing Iraq. US artillery was added to the Daguet Division's assets for the land offensive.

Bottom right :
The roof of a Humvee affords these US Marines better visibility in the flat desert, but at the cost of a dusty ride.

Firing line of US Marine
M60A1 tanks. The elderly
Pattons, up-graded with
reactive armor slabs,
remain more suitable for
some Marine missions than
the new generation of heavy
MBTs; nevertheless, their
successful battle for Kuwait
International Airport in
February will presumably
be the last taste of action for
these veterans.

Top left :
The hours tick away to H-Hour, and US Marine LVTP-7 amphibious tracked carriers move up to the Kuwaiti frontier, while allied aircraft pound enemy lines relentlessly.

Bottom left :
Less than a week before the ground assault, General Schwarzkopf deftly redeployed the weight of his front line forces to the north and west. Undetected by Irak, this manoeuvre enabled the stunningly successful 'left hook' by allied armor, airborne and mechanized units right across southern Irak to the Euphrates river. Here French VABs, which carried out the deepest penetration on the outside edge of the 'hook' alongside elements of the 82nd Airborne, move into position.

Top right :
US transport vehicles stalled by the kind of conditions which one does not readily associate with the sands of Araby : rain, cold, and clinging mud. The desert winter is brief but unmistakable.

Bottom right :
Tank tracks have a limited life, and commanders keep them on their enormous flat-bed transporters until the last possible minute : track-miles are an asset to be husbanded. Here Abrams tanks are moved up to the front on Saudi transporters, in one of the hundreds of convoys, totalling tens of thousands of vehicles, which alone made 'Desert Storm' possible. The war may have lasted only 100 hours; but General Schwarzkopf had stockpiled enough of everything for two month's fighting.

THE WAR
FIVE WEEKS AND A HUNDRED HOURS

At 2 a.m. on Sunday 24 February 1991 hundreds of thousands of troops and 3,000 tanks began to move forward into the lanes cleared in the Iraqi minefields. The liberation of Kuwait was at hand; in one sense, it had inexorably begun five weeks before.

Since the early hours of 17 January the US and allied air forces had methodically destroyed virtually every strategic target in Iraq and occupied Kuwait. Learning from past experience not only in Vietnam but also in Grenada and Panama, the Pentagon — and above all General Schwarzkopf, the architect of this victory — were determined that this operation should be orchestrated to the last detail.

There would be no improvisation : every Iraqi target would be listed, analysed, and given its place in the order of priority. Thousands of objectives, meticulously researched by every available intelligence-gathering resource, were pounded to destruction.

Day and night, the most sophisticated computer-guided and laser-targeted weapons struck home with uncanny precision, and the 'iron bombs' rained down. Methodically, the aerial steam-roller crushed Saddam's war-machine; then turned to throttle his lines of communication and supply; and finally, brought its terrible weight down on the enemy troops in the front lines.

But Norman Schwarzkopf's masterpiece of generalship lay in his succesful deception of the enemy over his intentions for the ground war. To the very end Saddam Hussein believed that the US forces would land on the coast of Kuwait. In fact, thanks to a masterly concealed deployment to the north-west by the bulk of the allied heavy divisions, the weight of the offensive fell on southern Iraq itself.

An enormous turning movement by XVIII Airborne Corps (101st Airborne and 24th Mechanized Divisions, and 3rd Cavalry Regiment, with flanking cover from 82nd Airborne and the French division) and VII Corps (1st Cavalry, 1st Infantry, and 1st, 3rd and 1st British Armored Divisions) — slashed across the rear of the enemy army in Kuwait, trapping it in a gigantic pocket and destroying its mobile reserves. The Iraqi army was faced with a stark choice : surrender, or be wiped out by allied armor and airpower.

On the night of 27 February the first soldiers of the free Kuwaiti army entered their capital. Seven months of cruel occupation were coming to an end. The coalition had won; and early on the morning of the 28th a unilateral ceasefire was declared, just one hundred hours after the offensive opened.

Previous page :
The Baghdad skyline during the first allied raids. Iraqi anti-aircraft artillery was very powerful, but was quickly reduced to more or less blind firing. Allied F-4G 'Wild Weasel' aircraft sought out and destroyed target acquisition radars, and communications were jammed by ECM aircraft.

Top left :
A slightly forced smile from the pilot of an A-10A Thunderbolt II tank-buster about to take off for a strike against enemy tanks around the Saudi border town of Khafji during the January fighting.

Bottom left :
One of the USAF 37th Tactical Fighter Wing's extraordinary F-117A 'Stealth' aircraft refuels in mid-flight. The F-117 struck the first blows of all against strategic Iraqi targets during the air raids of 17 January.

Top right :
Royal Air Force Tornado F.3 air superiority fighter over its Gulf base. The F.3s escorted their Tornado GR.1 bomber counterparts on the first long missions against Saddam's airfields, but the lack of aerial opposition robbed them of their primary task.

Bottom right :
French Jaguar fighter-bomber taking off from Al Ahsa air base. Despite their age these 'bomb trucks' carried out more than 1 000 sorties successfully, and without loss.

One of 48 US Marine Corps
F-18A Hornets deployed to
the Gulf, refuelling in
flight; rendezvous with
'flying gas stations'
extended the range of all
types of US strike aircraft,
allowing them to penetrate
every corner of Iraqi
airspace. This Hornet
served with VMFA-235 out
of Muharraq in Bahrain;
the Marine jets carried out
many missions over
Kuwait, with minimal
losses.

Weapons guidance screens
in allied aircraft recorded
'bomb's eye views' of many
Iraqi targets taken out with
pin-point accuracy by
means of laser designation :
here, munitions stores, a
strategic bridge, an Iraqi oil
tanker, and an oil terminal.
After a month of allied
raids it was only possible to
buy a tankful of gas in Iraq
— one of the world's major
oil-producers — for many
hundreds of dollars on the
black market.

Previous page :
A Tomahawk cruise missile blazes away from the battleship USS *Wisconsin* to begin its uncannily accurate computer-guided journey. It will hug the terrain for hundreds of miles, altering course at pre-programmed 'landmarks', until it arrives at an individually designated target building in Baghdad with a precision measured in feet.

Top left :
On its way to Iraq, an F-18 Hornet of Navy squadron VFA-192 above the carrier USS *Midway*.

Bottom left :
The thunder and the lightning... The 16-in. guns of the battleship USS *Wisconsin* pound Iraqi bunkers on the coast of Kuwait.

Top right :
The F-111F 'Aardvark' — here a pair named 'Lady Liberty I' and 'II' from the 48th Tactical Fighter Wing — played a major part in the destruction of Saddam's military-industrial complex.

Bottom right :
The destruction of Iraqi command centres, communications, utilities, militarily important factories, and transport choke-points continued 24 hours a day from the early hours of 17 January. Saddam's ability to supply or control his 42 divisions in Kuwait became more fatally degraded as each day passed.

Above :
While jets took out strategic targets, at tactical level the attack helicopter was king of the battlefield. Cobras and Apaches roamed under leaden winter skies, hungry for targets, and became the daily dread of the Iraqi troops.

Right :
US Marines examine a T-55 knocked out during the Iraqis' puzzlingly pointless thrust into the abandoned border town of Khafji in late January. It cost them at least two full battalions.

Opposite :
On 31 January US 3rd Marine Division gunners fired 155mm howitzers in support of Saudi and Qatari troops recapturing Khafji with Marine back-up.

Previous page :
Covered by a smoke-screen, M1 Abrams tanks of the 197th Infantry Brigade (Mechanized)(Separate) attached to XVIII Airborne Corps advance across the desert. The world's first gas turbine powered tank, the Abrams can cross flat country at 45 mph; its Chobham armor, overpressure NBC protection and fire suppression systems give its crews 'high survivability'; and its 105mm cannon with ultra-sophisticated fire control computers can achieve first-time hits with a probability of more than 90 per cent, day or night.

Top left :
82nd Airborne paratroopers take cover in the miserable winter conditions of January and February.

Bottom left :
The vital first step in any land offensive was the penetration of Iraqi minefields. One of several methods employed by the allies was a combination of 'flails' and 'ploughs' mounted on the hulls of tanks, to set off mines harmlessly, and to drag others to the surface where they could be marked, and dealt with at leisure. This is an AMX-30B2 tank of France's 4th Dragoons serving with the Daguet Division.

Overleaf :
The main allied armored thrust round the rear of the Iraqi defenses on 26-28 February was carried out by the US VII Corps. The British 1st Armoured Division took the right flank position, swooping south-east into the enemy rear. The three Challenger tank regiments provided the cutting edge of the British formation.

The central thrust into occupied Kuwait in February was made by Arab units of the coalition forces. Here men of the Egyptian 3rd Mechanized Division observe an Iraqi strongpoint before resuming their attack.

Top left :
MPs of the 82nd Airborne mark the new ownership of an Iraqi post on the morning of 24 February.

Below :
Crammed into their transport vehicles, the paratroopers of the 82nd drive deep into the Iraqi rear, not stopping even to take prisoners.

Opposite :
Serving alongside the US paratroopers, French Marine infantry of the 3rd RIMa snatch a brief meal during the joint column's amazing hundred-mile hook to the Euphrates in less than 36 hours.

Previous page :
The French AMX-30B2, though up-dated, is basically a last-generation tank; but any worries about sending them against Iraq's Soviet types proved unnecessary. In less than an hour they knocked out 20 enemy tanks and a couple of dozen other armored vehicles, without suffering loss or casualties; it took just 270 rounds of 105mm.

Top left :
Soviet-built MTLB armored troop carrier, brushed out of the path of the headlong left-flank advance by the Daguet Division and 82nd Airborne.

Bottom left :
Egyptian infantry of the 3rd Mechanized Division, equipped with US M113 carriers, fight their way closer to Kuwait City.

Opposite :
'Toms' of the British 7th Armoured Brigade's 1st Bn., Staffordshire Regiment. In the event the Iraqis surrendered, in their thousands, without forcing the British infantry to fight any major positional actions.

Overleaf :
Dawn advance by Warriors of the British division.
***Inset left :* Challengers of the Royal Scots Dragoon Guards. On 26 February, in the division's only major battle, the British tanks, artillery and multiple rocket launchers destroyed some 200 Iraqi tanks and overran the enemy 52nd Division in northern Kuwait.**
***Inset right :* 'Giant Viper' — a rocket-propelled hose charge fired over enemy minefields — clears a path 200 yards long and 20 feet wide in one massive explosion.**

Top left :
French Marines of the 3rd RIMa gather AK-47s dumped by thousands of Iraqi prisoners.

Bottom left :
British infantry pause in a rudimentary trench.

Top right :
US tankers of the 3rd Armored Division photographed during a halt deep inside Iraq.

Bottom right :
Foreign Legion sappers lift mines from the path of the advance near As Salman.

Previous page :
The XVIII Airborne Corps didn't stop for anything once they crossed the Iraqi border; resistance brought the briefest pause to check out enemy dispositions, then the armor and infantry rolled forward once more — over it, through it, round it... The M163 Vulcan 20mm rotary cannon mounted on this 'track' was originally intended for anti-aircraft protection, but proved an effective infantry support weapon too.

Left :
Even in victory, the 'dogfaces' are hard to impress. Tired, cold and ready for anything Saddam can throw at them, these GIs of the 'Big Red One' wait for their orders for the next bound forward.

Opposite top :
The turret of a Republican Guard T-72, totally destroyed by an anti-tank missile, on the Basra-Baghdad highway. Under a sky ruled by the American tactical air force Iraq's élite corps and most modern Soviet armor could not even organise a coherent resistance.

Opposite bottom :
Provisional estimates put Iraq's losses at 3,000 tanks and at least 2,000 other combat vehicles. If they stayed in their hides, allied armor came and found them; if they ran for home, the sky fell on them.

Previous page :
When allied mobile units encountered major enemy positions or troop concentrations they called in attack helicopters and self-propelled artillery. 82nd Airborne troopers take a break while an Iraqi vehicle concentration is 'sterilized'.

Top left :
Some of at least 70,000 Iraqi prisoners trudge past advancing artillery of the US XVIII Airborne Corps. They hardly needed guarding : in many cases their own field-grade officers told them to surrender at the first opportunity.

Bottom left :
French Marines stack captured weapons in the town of As Salman.

Top right :
GI of the '24th Mech', proud curator of a collection of Kalashnikovs taken from prisoners on the Basra-Baghdad highway.

Bottom right :
Pundits compared Saddam's Republican Guard to the Waffen-SS. By the time allied airpower had visited with the Guard's motorized columns they certainly resembled the aftermath of the Falaise pocket in 1944; in any other respect, the comparison was absurd.

Previous page :
The problem with a 'cult of personality' is that when you fail, you leave a lot of embarrassing souvenirs for the troops who call your bluff.

Top left :
Once a feared adversary, now a pile of abandoned scrap : an Iraqi ZPU-2 'triple-A' battery.

Bottom left :
Hungry, bewildered, abandoned by their leader, and traumatised by the allied onslaught, Iraqi troops seemed only too eager to give up in the hope of safety and a meal. Their treatment would be decent, even generous; but the initial humiliation was unavoidable, and no soldier could feel anything but pity for them.

Opposite :
A vehicle of the '24th Mech' flies a jaunty Jolly Roger as it cuts deep into southern Iraq.

The victor, and the vanquished. History offers no parallel for a war between armies each half a million strong, won in six weeks of air and four days of land combat, in which the winners suffered such miraculously low casualties. The GIs, Marines, and allied troopers, and their brothers-in-arms in the skies, have just smashed the world's fourth most powerful army at the cost of less than 200 dead and around 300 wounded.

PHOTO CREDITS

Yves Debay : front cover, 4, 7, 8 (bottom), 9, 10/11, 12 (bottom), 14, 15, 16/17, 19, 22, 23, 24 (top), 25, 26, 27, 28 (bottom), 29 (bottom), 31, 34 (bottom), 35, 36, 38, 39, 40 (bottom), 41, 43, 47, 50, 51, 52, 53, 54, 55, 58, 59, 60/61, 62 (top), 63, 66, 67, 70 (bottom), 71, 72/73, 74, 75 (top), 78 (bottom), 79, 80/81, 82, 83, 84/85, 87, 90 (top), 98 (top), 99, 100/101, 102, 103, 104/105, 106, 107, 108/109, 110, 114 (top), 115, 116/117, 118, 119, 120/121, 122, 123, 124/125, 126, 127, 128, 129, (plus back cover unless specified).

Eric Micheletti : 8 (top), 12 (top), 13, 20/21, 24 (bottom), 28 (top), 29 (top), 32/33, 34 (top), 37, 40 (top), 44/45, 46, 48/49, 56/57, 62 (bottom), 68/69, 70 (top), 76/77, 78 (top).

Will Fowler : 64/65, 75 (bottom), 112/113, 114 (bottom, *via*).
Ian Black : 91 (top).
AP/ Dominique Mollard : 88/89.
Department of Defense : 90 (bottom), 92/93, 97 (top).
US Navy : 96 (top).
British Ministry of Defence : 111.
French Air Force (SIRPA/AIR) : 91 (bottom), 92 (bottom).
John McCutcheon/Union Tribune Publishing Co. : 94/95.
Rex Features Ltd : 96 (bottom), 97 (bottom).
Christopher Morris, Black Star/Colorific! : 98 (bottom).

© 1991 Eric Micheletti & Yves Debay
Printed in the United States of America

This edition published in
Great Britain 1991 by
Windrow & Greene Ltd.
5 Gerrard St., London W1V 7LJ

Design by François Vauvillier and
Jean-Marie Mongin/Histoire & Collections, Paris

British Library Cataloguing in Publication Data
Micheletti, Eric
    Victory in the Gulf
    1. Middle East. Wars, history, 1973-
    I. Title II. Debay, Yves
    954.6
ISBN 1-872004-31-8

Available from the same publisher :
'Operation Desert Shield : The first 90 days'
(64 pages : £9.95 UK, $15.95 USA
ISBN 1-872004-01-6)

Coming shortly :
'Air War Over The Gulf'
(64 pages : £ 9.95 UK, $15.95 USA
ISBN 1-872004-21-0)